Our forests and jungles are full of wild animals. They play in the trees and build nests among the branches. They munch on the leaves and hide in the shadows.

But some of these animals are in trouble. Too many of them are being hunted. Others are losing their homes. People are cutting the trees down. They are building cities and roads in the special places where animals like to live. Many of these **endangered species** might disappear from the earth forever.

In this book you will read about a few of the animals that need our help. They live in forests and jungles all over the world. Some of them are large and bold. Others are tiny and timid. Some are beautiful. A few are funny-looking. But each one is interesting and special in its own way.

The forest is a perfect hiding place for a **tiger**. With its orange fur and black stripes, it almost seems to disappear among the trees and tall grasses.

A female tiger is called a tigress. She's a fierce hunter, but she's also a good mother. A tigress will hide her small cubs away from danger in a cave or in thick bushes. When they are bigger and stronger, the tigress will teach her cubs how to be brave hunters just like her.

VANISHING ANIMALS OF THE JUNGLE AND FOREST

Lydia Bailey

Illustrations by

Olena Kassian

Scholastic Canada Ltd.

Scholastic Canada Ltd.
123 Newkirk Road, Richmond Hill, Ontario, Canada L4C 3G5

Scholastic Inc.
730 Broadway, New York, NY 10003, USA

Ashton Scholastic Pty Limited
PO Box 579, Gosford, NSW 2250, Australia

Ashton Scholastic Limited
Private Bag 1, Penrose, Auckland, New Zealand

Scholastic Publications Ltd.
Villiers House, Clarendon Avenue, Leamington Spa,
Warwickshire CV32 5PR, UK

We are grateful to Susan M. Woodward, Ross MacColloch, Mark Peck, and Dael E. Morris of the Royal Ontario Museum for their assistance in the preparation of this book.

6 5 4 3 2 1   Printed in Hong Kong   3 4 5 6 7/9

Canadian Cataloguing in Publication Data
Bailey, Lydia
    Vanishing animals of the jungle and forest

(Vanishing animals of the world)
ISBN 0-590-73071-1

1. Endangered species - Juvenile literature.
2. Jungle fauna - Juvenile literature. I. Kassian,
Olena. II. Title. III. Series.

QL112.B34 1993   j591.52'9   C92-094939-8

The next time you're walking through the woods and you hear what sounds like a dog barking, don't look down. Look up. It just might be a **spotted owl** that you hear! This round-headed, brown-eyed owl makes a call that sounds like a small dog barking. It goes like this: *Oh-ooh-oou-ooOWW!*

How good are a spotted owl's eyes and ears? Very good! When it's sitting at the top of a tall tree, this owl can see and hear a tiny mouse squeaking far below on the forest floor.

Aaaa-roooooo! Aaaa-rooooooo! A **red wolf** throws its head back, points its nose to the sky and howls at the moon. Soon other wolves join in and the wild howling really gets going.

Wolves don't need telephones. They keep in touch with each other by howling. People don't know all the reasons why wolves howl. Sometimes they want to tell the rest of the pack where they are. Other times they're saying they've found food. Or maybe it's because howling with friends on a moonlit night can be a whole lot of fun!

If someone asked you how big a hippo was, you would probably say it was huge! So you might be surprised to learn that one kind of hippo is smaller than you think. Unlike its larger cousin, the **pygmy hippopotamus** is about the size of a very big pig.

Pygmy hippos live alone in the darkest part of the jungle. At night they walk slowly through special jungle paths, contentedly munching on fruit and tender green plants. In the deepest part of the jungle these paths are like tunnels through the thick leaves. Imagine having your supper in a leafy green tunnel!

Hissssssss! A mother **python** is sitting on her eggs, and she doesn't want anyone to bother them. She coils her long body around nearly 100 eggs and rests her head on top. This is how she makes sure they stay warm and snug.

When it's time for a baby python to be born, it breaks a hole through its leathery egg with a little egg tooth. Then out it slides and away it goes. Baby pythons don't need to stay with their mothers. Unlike human babies, they can take care of themselves from the minute they're born.

If you ever meet a **mountain gorilla** on a jungle path, don't worry. Gorillas may be big and strong, but they are also gentle and peaceful. They just want to be left alone.

Every day, gorilla families travel through forests high up in the mountains. There they eat plants, take naps and lie around in the warm sun. Young gorillas find it hard to sit still while their parents are resting. They like to run around and play noisy games with each other. Sometimes dad gets mad and tells them to be quiet — in gorilla language, of course!

What animal looks like a little dinosaur? The
giant armadillo does. This animal may be timid and shy,
but it doesn't have to be. When it goes for a walk, an
armadillo is protected by its own suit of armour. A coat of
bony plates completely covers the top and sides of its body.

If an armadillo meets an enemy, it doesn't fight. Instead it
tries to roll up into a ball. Other times when it doesn't feel
safe, it does just what you might do. It runs away as fast as
its little legs will carry it.

Have you ever seen a butterfly as large as a bird? If your answer is no, then you've probably never seen the amazing **Queen Alexandra's birdwing**. This butterfly is the largest and heaviest butterfly in the whole world.

Birdwing butterflies fly high above the ground. They like to live in the tops of tall, tall trees. A male birdwing looks like a flying rainbow, with its bright yellow body and shining wings of yellow, green, blue and black. The beautiful colours warn enemies to stay away. These butterflies taste terrible. Their colours say: Look at me, but don't eat.

Imagine sleeping in a different bed every night of the week! **Orangutans** do just that. By day, they swing through the trees looking for fruit to munch. But when the sun starts to go down, they use branches and leaves to build themselves soft beds high up in the trees. An orangutan builds a new nest almost every night. There it sleeps, warm and safe and dry.

An orangutan baby stays close to its mother. It holds on tightly to her fur as she swings through the branches. When it rains, mom can keep them both dry by using a big green leaf as an umbrella.

Have you ever wondered what it would be like to stay up all night long? **Aye-ayes** don't have to wonder. They know. They spend most of the day curled up in little balls, asleep. But when the sun goes down and the forest is dark, the little aye-ayes wake up. They leap about in the trees looking for food.

Aye-ayes have amazingly long fingers and toes. The middle finger is the longest of all. Aye-ayes use that finger for almost everything. They reach into tree-holes with it to scoop out juicy insects for dinner. They also scratch with it, comb their coats with it and even use it to clean inside hard-to-reach places like their ears.

Once thousands of **Carolina parakeets** lived in the forests of North America. Now, sadly, there's not a single one left. This playful little green and yellow parrot has become **extinct**. It has disappeared from our earth forever.

Although we must say goodbye to the Carolina parakeet, the other animals in this book are still with us. It is true that their numbers are getting smaller. But we can save them. If we all work together and if we all care enough, we can make sure that these endangered animals are with us for a long, long time.